just love's way

just love's way

ATHENEUM SMITH
EDITED BY GRACE F. PENNER

Epigraph Books
Rhinebeck, New York

Just Love's Way © 2020 by Atheneum Smith

All rights reserved. No part of this book may be used or reproduced in any manner without the consent of the author, except in critical articles or reviews. Contact the publisher for information.

Paperback ISBN 978-1-951937-61-4
Hardcover ISBN 978-1-951937-65-2

Library of Congress Control Number 2020916503

Book design by Colin Rolfe

Epigraph Books
22 East Market Street
Suite 304
Rhinebeck, NY 12572
(845) 876-4861
epigraphps.com

Dedicated to Cindy and Lorraine

contents

just love's way	1
friends	2
maybe	3
not for a second	4
quest	5
face to face	6
let go of the best	7
just a memory	8
say you love me, only me	9
I love you	10
there is only one	11
captured	12
never	13
a sailor song	14
uncertain times	15
one day	16
the question	17
love will bridge the gap	18
ghost	19
red shoes	20
power	21
please	22
flowers' friend	23
without uttering a word	24
a warning	25
it was you	26
as good as you	27
guests at your table	28
everyone	29
my love is laughing	30
now let me dry your tears	31
leaf painter	32
my one last kiss	33

why	34
now you do	35
now you do, how can this be	36
how can you love the wind	37
the house's money	38
all alone this night	39
love's dimensions	40
immortal	41
if you live a lie	42
all the coins I can carry	43
among us	44
visitor	45
I see it in the distance	46
dreams	47
farewell	48
love's journey—editor's note	49
about the author	50

just love's way

leaves fall from the trees
it is neither bad nor good
it is for us to learn
it is just their way

the night follows the day
it is neither bad nor good
it is for us to learn
it is just that way

your dying
follows your living
it is neither bad nor good
it is for us to learn
it is just that way

love does not stray
love will never go away
it is for us to learn
it is just love's way

f r i e n d s

where do friends come from
the meeting seems so accidental
our need is unspoken
yet they hear us
in our loneliness
they find us

I understand but could you tell me
who are they
how will I know them

when the sun goes down
the world grows dark
your world grows dark

when you look
for something, anything
to hold onto

the arms that move around you
that embrace you
will lead you
to your friends

m a y b e

moments lost
moments gone
I could have been loving
I could have been strong

I will try again
I will find those friends of long ago
the ones I did wrong
who knows maybe

yesterday was yesterday
today is today
I have something to say
who knows maybe

they will understand
these words of love
being sent their way
    maybe

not for a second

do not think for a second
that I am not concerned
or sympathetic

when I see
so many faces
looking back at me
eyes wondering
what will become of us

voices neither high nor low
voices speaking without words
how many of us are going to go

now if I can shoot
from my mind's quiver
a group of words

like arrows that strike you
then change the contours of your face
from fearful to cheerful

believe me when I say
I will not hesitate
not for a second

q u e s t

for most people it is their hope
to meet the one they love

for me it is my hope
to love every one I meet

most will think
my quest will
end in defeat

however, I must try

face to face

please forgive me
most I cannot change
yet I can shed my tears
in the hope they will
stand in the way of your fears

you are so concerned with dying
If you can believe it
dying is not death

have you not heard
of the greatest house
with many rooms

walk through that door
find yourself
in a new place
where love dwells

If you can believe it
we will meet again
face to face

let go of the best

there was an argument
who do I love best
do I love you the best

or you over there
or you there in the back
or you in the front
or you standing next to me

do you not understand
there is no the best
love is sufficient unto itself
when you have one's love
you have all they can give

believe me in this
you do not want my strongest love
for my strongest love is set aside
reserved for certain people

for the people who hate me
believe me, those people you do not want to be

we should all be satisfied
just to be loved
if love is all there is
how can you have more
let go of the best

just a memory

just a memory
from my past
just a memory
how it lasts

I look back
at moments
moments so dark
compared to me
even a blind man could see

her kindness
her love
towards me

made me feel
there just might be
a little good left
inside of me

just a memory
from my past
inside of me

the memory will always remain
inside of me

say you love me, only me

a most difficult thing to see
the difficult part of me
if you really understand me
or when you get mad at me

one of the hardest things to do
scariest things to do
in this life
say those three words
I love you

my love, please say those words to me
words I long to hear
words just for me
say you love me, only me
do not tell me
there are two, three, four or even more

you do not know what you ask
what you ask, I cannot do
can't you see
I tell the truth
what you ask cannot be done
my heart tells me
all of us
are one

I love you

I have a question
for you
for me

what do we do
with these feelings
in our heart
when our heart
is breaking in two

put them in a cupboard
or up on a shelf
or bury them in the ground
so they cannot be found

I suppose that is why
love has a lonely heart
because we bury
so many of our feelings
where they can never be found

I suppose that is a good reason
for you and me
to say
I love you

there is only one

artist easel standing ready
clip on the paper
the day's work has begun

add water to the pigments
a wash here
an overlay there
shapes and forms
start to appear

then to one side
you notice two distinct colors
moving towards
each other

how very close they have become
in an instant
one realizes
there are no longer
two different colors
there is only one

c a p t u r e d

could I have been mistaken
he is here, he came
with a love
from who knows where
maybe I am not forsaken

not easy to grasp
has taken me a lifetime
to convince myself
I will not be loved

I walked through his door
I am standing on new ground
all the rules have changed

I have to decide
this love, which way to go
a strange feeling comes over me

I am caught in his net
he has captured me
his love is never going
to let me go

n e v e r

don't you see don't you see
what you say
is just confusing me, confusing me

you say this
then you say that
you are confusing me

is love this
or is love that
you are confusing me

understand love is this
understand love is that
how can that be, tell me how can that be

listen, listen, closely now to me
love is this, love is that

love is the beginning, love is the end
here is the answer, it is simple

love has no beginning, love has no end
love is forever
love will never go away
never

a sailor song

lips upon the water
salt in the air
feelings of love
come from who knows where

like boats upon the shore
waiting for the wind
we look to love
to take us
to places we have never been

with sails raised high
gazing into the sky
happy you are here with me
sweet dear blue eyes

uncertain times

uncertain times are they
whenever traveling to new places
it is to be expected
anxiety and fear will hitch a ride

be suspicious
let them not become your guide
instead let love blaze your trail
how many times must I say
it will not fail

now let me repeat the news
he who is fond of his life
that one, he is the one who will lose

mumbling the crowd always mumbling
what else could they do
when I keep speaking
as I do
about things they consider insane

that life is so very good
but even still
dying is gain

o n e   d a y

are you serious
could you not know
the battle has been fought
the battle has been won

the power the might
that turns
day into night

compared to love
evil is but a speck
trying to find its place
next to the sun

a necessary speck
you took your sight for granted
the speck came and took your sight away
your sight will be returned

returned to you one day
then we will see
if you take
your sight for granted anymore

the question

my thoughts and feelings
you now possess
you have them
you have me

you know me
you realize
you are safe with me
I will protect you

you know me
standing by your side
no one will hurt you
you are safe with me

when you are standing next to me
you look at me
I look at you
we both ask the question

who will protect your heart
from me

love will bridge the gap

for your love to be fulfilled and complete
one does not need
to be with the person they love

all that is needed
is to put your faith in that love
believe and know it is true
love will bridge the gap

nothing for you to do
nothing for you to say
let love show you the way
love will bridge the gap

time and space have met their match
love can move so quickly without a trace
time and space it can erase

from here to there
from there to here
any time   all the time
　　before time   after time
love will bridge the gap

g h o s t

mind and heart
come inside
if you wish to see

how I think
how I love
beautiful feelings
insecure thoughts

days so bright
nights so blue
wishing I could always
be with you

then wondering
if we might belong
to others in our past
from long ago

red shoes

red building
red vest
I have been looking so long
I need a rest

I try, it doesn't matter
I haven't a clue
what am I to do

maybe I can help
I think you have the key
to unlock the door
to find what you are looking for

it is just this simple
close your eyes
now make that wish
now click those red shoes three times

open your eyes, now what do you see
just an old man taking this picture of me
ask him   go ahead   ask him

mister, is there a chance you could help me
it is just this simple my dear, that is what
makes the treasure so difficult to see
it can only reside in one place
    inside thee

power

the cup we demand
will leave us thirsty

the hand we command
will not lighten our load

the loyalty we expect
is slavery

the affection we desire
will leave us lonely

love looks on in silence

p l e a s e

I think I love you
I think you love me
but I do not understand
why then, do you displease me so

displease you, how did I displease you?
you did this, then you did that
you were like this, then you were like that

can't you see, how you displease me
why can't you be more like this
then you could be more like that
I wish you were more like this
I wish you were more like that

I can make your wish come true
for you, I can do this, for you
I can be more like this, for you
I can be more like that, for you
for you, for you, I can do this, for you

then I would like for you
to do something for me, please
just say these words
for me, please, these words, please

I do not love you
I love someone that I want you to be
I do not love you
I love someone that I want you to be
I think, I think
that is what, I want, I think

flowers' friend

the wind such a thing
have you seen it wrap its fingers
around the flowers in your garden

the wind gathers up the fragrance
takes it away
to wherever it wishes
I do not think the flowers
have lost a thing

without uttering a word

looking back
I did not know
you talk every place you go
without uttering a word

the way you move
the way you stand
a slight movement of your hand
lets me inside

try as you may
your feelings
you cannot hide

I did not mean to look
I did not mean to see
oh well
I saw your tell

I saw your secrets
all you try to hide
you try to hide
deep inside

can't you see
you keep talking to me
without uttering a word

a warning

days so long ago
now it seems
just a bad dream

drunken days
drunken nights
not coming home
till the morning light

broken dishes
broken promises
broken hearts

what was I thinking
not much
just feeling how an empty heart
could be so full
of pain

I have plenty
I am a guy
who likes to share

get too close
after I am done
your heart will need repair
I warned you

it was you

words moving in my mind
I direct them to my heart
write down these lines
for someday you might find

loving eyes looking at me
then a moment goes by
the eyes change

now they are crying
full of pain
full of tears

that will happen
stay with me ten years

but take heart, if ever you ask
where was the love
it is right here with me
do you not recognize it
I stole it from you

but now my work is almost done
so I will send it back to the one
who changed a dark heart
into the sun,
it was you

as good as you

my friend
there was so much
so very much
you could not do

change a light bulb
hang a picture
drive a nail
you would try
but you would fail

I saw it all
I was always there
I was a friend
friends do what their friends cannot do

then I would look at all my other friends
see all the many things they can do
then it was your time to die
I was with you
with you to your last seconds alive

now I wonder
if my friends will do
as good as you
when it is their time to die
will they come close to doing
as good as you

guests at your table

the grain that is crushed
so often places itself before the wheel
for the wheat that is turned into flour
knows its destiny is to become
your evening meal

the heat from the fire transforms
the dough into something greater
than itself

the temper and the aggressive nature of
the controlling transforms the meek
and lowly into royalty

I wonder after the food has been eaten
the bread is all gone
do the guests at your table
ever realize
the kindness they consumed
was love not weakness

e v e r y o n e

think you are separate
think you are alone
I agree

we are all separate
like leaves on a tree
our ego does this
to you, to me

a leaf here another there
then it happens
a strange thought
could it be

we are part of something
greater than you
greater than me
could it be

we are not separate
we are not alone
we are one
everyone

a part of the tree

my love is laughing

my love laughs
has it been more than fifty years
has it really been that long
well who would have guessed, except me
my love for you would still be so strong

I drove by, was it by chance
not a chance, it was meant to be
I was at your crash
all that bent metal, that took you away
took you away so fast

my love laughs, fifty years
try if you can
get your mind around this thought

my love is forever, now that is something
time has never seen
my love just laughs, when I look down
at the small stone in the ground
with your name, flowers I planted all around

my love laughs, yet then I wonder
why am I always crying
whenever I think of those moments
when you were dying

you have gone away
but my heart senses
you are right next to me
I suppose that is why

my love is laughing

now let me dry your tears

close your eyes
now let me touch you
let me touch you softly

feel me   feel me
against your cheeks
let me run my fingers
through your hair

do not be afraid
if you cry
I will dry your tears

my moves are so graceful
you will not hear me coming
you will not hear me leaving

my moves are legendary
I have become famous
famous in my own time
famous for all time

if you want to call me
call me by my name
    warm breeze
now let me dry your tears

leaf painter

he was here last night
came right into town, he did
painted all the trees different colors
got some people mad at him

geese flying overhead today
I was working on a barn
I heard them talking to each other
leaf painter look he has been around
flying so high they see more than I

squash and pumpkins laying in the garden
old and lazy
yellow, gold and orange
they moved around in the summer
but now they are too fat

someone stole the faces off my sunflowers
I went to look for them
but empty seeds were all I found

I saw some birds smiling at me
I think they took my faces
or it could have been leaf painter

my one last kiss

I look around my room
focus on the door people walking in
a look on their faces

they are not prepared, not ready
what to say what to do
I wonder if they are aware
that their eyes just stare

then one, maybe two people who know
they take control not with force or might
they touch me, they touch me just right
oh that feeling it feels so right

in a room with the dying
you would think the energy would be low
that is not what I sense
I feel the power, the power of dying

fading I am going
one last gesture
no strength left even in my lips
my mind will have to blow

my final kiss
to those who love me
my one last kiss

w h y

living in the country on an old farm
has its own personal charm
my hands carve wood
or does wood carve me

sitting down
at the end of the day
I feel the wisp
of the summer wind
against my skin

look up into the sky
just ask why
this good life has come to me
why this woman is beside me

why the kingdom of heaven
has come to rest in me
    love only knows

now you do

so young, we met, in a library
we drove to the river, you sat next to me
then in parking lot, I saw you, you saw me

you were behind a desk, I came to see
divorce papers that day, sad feeling, I came to see

apartment by the river
held you close, you held me
we were two ghosts
nothing to hold on to
nothing for you, nothing for me

sending feelings over a lifetime
through the air, never landing
for you to share

I always knew, some day
I would see you
look into your eyes and say
I love you

thinking you will say
if only I knew
I will say
now you do

now you do, how can this be

can someone tell me
how can this be

a fleeting moment
a chance encounter
a stolen night

this love
really had no beginning
this love, a mere firefly of light

a few moments in my youth
now please tell me
how can this be

this love
which had no beginning
I now find
has no ending

can someone, please tell me
how can this be

how can you love the wind

when the wind touches your skin
with a hand soft and gentle remember me

when walking in the open air
and there is stillness in your heart
the trees will tell you, I have gone
remember me and someday I will return
to make the leaves in your heart dance

when walking by the sea remember me
the salt air tells you, all of me is not sweet

when you see the wind bringing in dark clouds
remember me, for as I carry rain to you
I also have to let the droplets pass through me
in your sorrow you are not alone

when the sails on the boats are dropped
people batten down their houses, in fear of the coming storm
remember me and the force and power of my love

when the sun returns
the sky is clear and the air clean, remember me
and the purity of our love

when you try to speak or show people my love
know beforehand your failure
for though they may see the wind's effects
its essence is invisible

better to tell them, to find the depth of love
in their own hearts, to understand mine
for how can you love the wind

the house's money

we started out
not knowing
how this would turn out

who can predict
how love will go
every relationship is a gamble

all you can do is put your money down
then hope for the best
win, place, or show

but no one forced us to the track
we picked our horse
so who can you blame
if you don't come in
win, place, or show

I have my own personal point of view
this gambling with love
for win, place, or show

I never gave it a second thought
like I said, I walked into this track
put my money down

didn't care about
win, place, or show
didn't even care if I came in last

for with love, it may sound funny
I always thought I was playing
with the house's money

all alone this night

alone, all alone this night
the arms of her memories
wrap around her, and hold her tight

these will be the only arms
around her this night
she would like to be wrong
just this one night

but here she is, tasting her tears
the taste   tells her
this is the way, it will be tonight

her memory is her memory
a sad old house for her thoughts
and her thoughts can work for her
as easily as they work against her

she remembers there was a love
who said
I do not have to be there, to be here

he said he loved her that day
and all of her tomorrows
is not today one of those tomorrows
he said he loved her
not who she was
not what she was, he said he loved her

now this lonely night
her tears taste a little sweeter
she is alone
but not all alone, this night

love's dimensions

please tell me
what is the depth
of a vessel
which has no bottom

can you tell me
when we speak a sound
or shine a light
how far they travel

can you tell me
love's dimensions
could it be
the measure of one's love
is in proportion
to one's ability to forgive

will I forgive you
will you forgive me
we shall see

immortal

the young tree said to the rock
old rock what is immortality
the old rock said
when you are an old rock
when I am a young tree
ask me this question again
but for now let the birds sing in you
let the rain drops drip off your leaves
let the sun rays warm you
let the winter winds freeze you
let be what is this day
for this very moment is immortal

if you live a lie

I told a lie
I am not sure why
I guess my ears
did not want to hear
what I had done
who I had become

so then I became the lie
those around me
did not know me
they only knew the lie

people came by
they were gracious
they did not talk to me
they just talked to the lie

what hurt most
the people I loved
the people closest to me
no longer talked to me
only to the lie

if you tell a lie
your fate, your destiny
will be like mine
if you live a lie

you become that lie
no one will know you
they will only know the lie

lonely you will be

all the coins I can carry

there was a man
he slipped a coin into his pocket
one coin
two sides

one side was love
one side was pain
for him
they had become the same

he walked into a bank
he had a decision to make
teller teller
give me all the coins
give me all the coins I can carry

when walking home
he fell three times
what is one to expect
it was a heavy load

in his life
love and pain
had become the same
give me all the coins I can carry

among us

there is one
who walks among us
give him no name
the last thing he seeks
is fortune or fame

a glance here
a smile there
those who have heart
can feel he is near

he quietly sows his seeds
without you knowing it
they grow and fulfill your dreams
the one who walks among us

the moon appears
then disappears
time melts away
like ice on a sunny day

he walks among us
speaks under his breath
so no one can hear
I will always love you
as he walks among us

visitor

I have a wife
people ask me about her

I tell them what I can
she is a loner
yet often
does not like to be alone

she likes the outside of people
but cares more about the inside

they ask me where is she from
not from around here I say
from far far away

the place where she comes from
I have heard these people referred
to as aliens

I do not use that word
when I speak softly to myself
I call her
    angel

I see it in the distance

almost invisible
after all this time
it has only taken a lifetime

I see it in the distance
who else can see it
can anyone see me running

running always running
often falling, much of my journey
my time was spent crawling

my mind is having trouble
I can no longer discern
what is real

I just sense things
as if I had no eyes
my feelings are my guide

I see it in the distance
who else can see it
the end of the race
the end of the wire

I just keep running
because I am a man on fire

d r e a m s

winter is here
light snow falling

dreams move you so quickly to the ocean
warm sand beneath your feet

count all the grains of sand
when you are through
you will discover
I still love you

f a r e w e l l

you should know
if you hold on
if you let go
my love remains

love's journey

one year ago
we would never have thought
we would be here
writing these final words
what do we mean by final?
were we on a journey
and this is our last day
was it a place we visited
and this is the last train stop
was it a time in our life we shared
and the clock has run out
or is it simply the end of a book about love
    and final really means beginning

Grace F. Penner, editor

about the author

The author is an artisan surrounded by a loving family and friends in the beautiful Hudson Valley. This collection of poems expresses his abstract reflections from a lifetime of personal experiences and lessons learned from others about love. All told, the mystery of love, he believes, is *just love's way*.